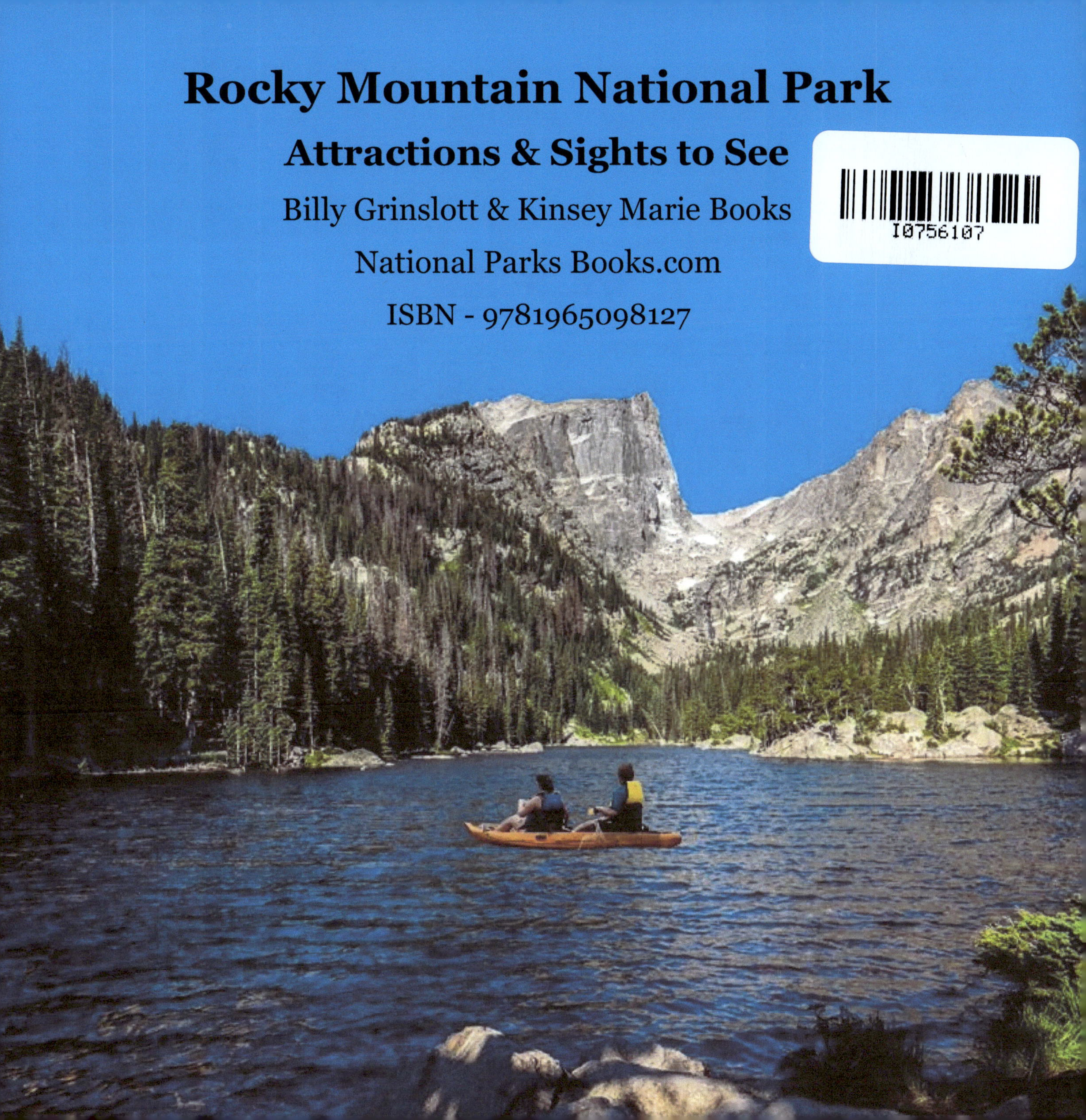
Rocky Mountain National Park
Attractions & Sights to See
Billy Grinslott & Kinsey Marie Books
National Parks Books.com
ISBN - 9781965098127
I0756107

There are many things to do in the Rocky Mountain National Park. We have Listed the most popular sites to see.

Rocky Mountain National Park has over 60 mountain peaks that are over 12 thousand feet high. The tallest is Longs Peak at 14,259 feet. That's 2.7 miles high.

Trail Ridge Road is the number one way to drive through the Rocky Mountains. The road is 48 miles long. Eleven miles of this highway travel above tree line and offers great views of the mountains. Trail Ridge Road, U.S. 34 offers excellent views, all from the comfort of your car.

From the Bear Lake parking area, a quarter mile walk on a marked path will take you to Bear Lake itself. Bear Lake offers spectacular scenic views of ponderosa pines, Bear Lake, Hallett Peak, and surrounding mountain peaks. Bear Lake is one of the most popular areas in the park. Bear Lake parking area fills up early in the day, often by 10 am each day. The trail is wheelchair accessible and has learning signs along the way.

Adams Falls Enjoy this 0.8-mile roundtrip trail near Grand Lake, Colorado. Generally considered an easy route. Adams Falls is a towering waterfall that eventually feeds into Grand Lake. Adams falls is outside the park entry near grand lake. The area is quite beautiful. The trail is a bit steep in places.

Chasm Falls is a cool little waterfall that cuts right through the surrounding rock, creating a narrow, fast flowing water display. Easiest way to get to it is from old Fall River Road. Along Old Fall River Road, use a pull out to park and walk 1 mile down to Chasm Falls.

Alberta Falls. You'll get great views of the surrounding peaks. This scenic hike is also one of the most popular. This scenic 30-foot waterfall rushes down a narrow gorge on and offers hikers an excellent spot to enjoy a relaxing picnic. Distance: 1.2 miles round trip.

Ouzel Falls. This easy 2.7-mile hike one-way passes by three other waterfalls and several other smaller cascades. Ouzel Falls runs over a cliffside that has huge boulders, making it one of the most beautiful waterfalls in the rocky mountain national park.

Sprague Lake. Hiking distance is 0.7 miles round trip. This gorgeous, wheelchair and stroller accessible trail is great for hikers of all abilities. There are plenty of benches and lookouts over the lake to enjoy the views. Enjoy the view of mountain peaks clearly from the east shoreline. Sprague Lake is a great place to see a variety of wildlife. If you feel like walking around the lake, you can.

Emerald Lake hiking distance is 4.1 miles round trip. The trail goes by other lakes, before reaching Emerald Lake. In a half-mile, you will reach Nymph Lake, a charming lake filled with blooming pond lilies. Another half-mile hike, you will reach Dream Lake. From here Emerald Lake is about another mile with steady elevation gain. If you enjoy viewing lakes, this hike is well worth it.

The Alluvial Fan is a beautiful cascade of water flowing down through a boulder field. In the Fall, the changing foliage of aspen groves are some of the most dramatic in the park, be sure to bring a camera. Explore this 0.7-mile roundtrip trail. This is a very popular area for hiking and walking. This short trail explores this massive collection of rocks where the Roaring River enters Horseshoe Park.

Lily Lake walking distance is 0.8 miles round trip. Lily Lake Loop is a level path with awesome views and is for visitors of all abilities. Take in views of Longs Peak, the Meeker Mountains, and Twin Sisters Mountains. There are several benches and picnic tables around the lake. You can also fish in this area. Hike up the ridge trail if you want an aerial view of the lake.

Dream Lake hiking distance 2.2 miles round trip. This is a very popular area for fishing, hiking, and snowshoeing, so you'll likely encounter other people while exploring. This short and easy hike takes you to some pristine and beautiful alpine lakes. Discover the tranquility of Dream Lake, with its crystal-clear waters reflecting the surrounding mountain peaks.

Sky Pond. At roughly 4.5 miles of hiking, you will arrive at Sky Pond, which sits at an elevation of 10,900 feet. The trail is long and hard. There are a lot of rocks in the trail and some scramble. It's a long hike so ensure you're staying hydrated.

At 14,259 feet, Longs Peak towers above all other summits in the Rockies. This mountain is seen from almost anywhere in the park. When conditions allow, thousands climb to Longs summit via the Keyhole Route. The Keyhole Route is not a hike. It is a climb that crosses enormous sheer vertical rock faces, often with falling rocks. The route has narrow ledges, loose rock, and steep cliffs. For most of the year, climbing to Longs Peak is in winter conditions, which requires winter mountaineering experience and the knowledge and use of specialized equipment.

On the east side of Rocky Mountain National Park, is a lesser explored area called the Wild Basin. The hikes in the Wild Basin take you to multiple waterfalls, up to alpine lakes, snowfields, and hidden areas of Rockies very few travelers see. This 5.3-mile out-and-back trail is considered a moderately challenging route and offers a variety of sightseeing opportunities.

Lake Haiyaha appears green at times, because of the way the lake absorbs and reflects the sunlight, it will look milky green at times. This four-mile roundtrip, moderately difficult hike passes three lakes, Bear, Nymph and Dream. Before the trail ends at Lake Haiyaha. About 50 yards from the lake the terrain gives way to rugged boulders covering the entire shore. Carefully navigate this area, the rocks can be slippery.

Bierstadt Lake. It’s a moderate hike up a mile with many switchbacks. Add in the elevation and it could be very difficult for many. The lake itself is surrounded by marsh so there is very little access to get right to the water. An easy trail goes around the lake so you can see it from multiple spots. It's not one of the more scenic hikes, but the views at the lake are good.

Get panoramic views of Rocky Mountain National Park from Many Parks Curve Overlook. Along the trail ridge road, use this pull out to see the low-land meadows. Moraine Park, upper beaver meadows, and horseshoe park meadows. They are all visible with deer mountain and Longs peak in the background.

Chasm Lake offers spectacular views of Longs Peak, the highest peak in the park. The lake sits below Longs Peak. The hike is a Distance of 4.2 miles one-way. The elevation for this climb starts at 9400 feet and goes up 2,390 feet from there. Recommended for experienced and in shape hikers. The altitude is high and will be stressful conditions for most hikers.

West Horseshoe Park Pullout. Has some great views and can be used to access the surrounding horseshoe park meadow. **Upper Horseshoe Meadow Pullout.** Use this pullout to see views of Horseshoe Park meadows and the Mummy Mountain Range. Bighorn Sheep, Moose, and Elk in the meadow below can be spotted from this location.

Mills Lake hiking Distance is 5 miles round trip. Hike past waterfalls, along streambeds, and above a glacially carved gorge. Enjoy great views of Longs Peak, Keyboard of the Winds, and Pagoda Mountain from Mills Lake. The last third of the hike crosses many big rock slabs and following the trail can be a little difficult at times.

Deer Mountain is 10,013 feet tall and surrounded by a forest with sweet smelling ponderosa pines. Switchbacks ease hikers to the summit. At the summit, you are rewarded with views of Longs peak, Moraine park, Upper beavers meadows, and Estes park. Be wary of thunderstorms, check the weather before hiking this trail. Deer Mountain is one of the most lightning struck mountains in the park. The trail is 6-miles roundtrip, considered a moderately challenging route.

Flattop mountain is 12,324 feet tall, the trail runs along the continental divide. This trail is well marked and well used. But this trail is one of the most difficult. You will get incredible views of Dream lake, Bear Lake, and Hallet peak. As well as the opportunity to stand on the nation's dividing continental line. Distance: 8.8 miles round trip, challenging, strenuous.

Take a hike on the Tundra Communities Trail and experience awesome mountain views and the alpine tundra. High winds and cold temperatures limit what plants can grow here. Most alpine plants are perennials. Many plants are small, but their new blossoms may be full-sized. The flowers that bloom, can take decades to do so. Also check out the Mushroom Rocks formations composed of gneiss and Silver. Hiking Distance is 1.2 miles round trip, considered an easy trail.

Sheep Lakes offers a scenic view. Carved out by glaciers, this beautiful area is a great place to view wildlife. The area is named for the bighorn sheep that come down from the mountainside to feed. You can also see coyotes, ground squirrels, and elk. Sheep Lakes is popular during the fall time when the animal's group up. There is no hiking involved, it is a roadside attraction.

Gem Lake is hidden and tucked away in the vast field of granite domes that located in the Lumpy Ridge area. Gem Lake is a shallow pond filled in by snowmelt and rainfall. The Gem Lake trail is accessed via the Lumpy Ridge Trailhead. The low elevation and southern sun exposure of the Gem Lake Trail make this a great year-round hike. Take in the views of Estes Park, Longs Peak, and the Continental Divide along this trail. Hiking distance: 3.4 miles roundtrip.

The Cub Lake Trail is a 4.6-mile round-trip hike. Along this trail you can see meadows, wildflowers, and water areas. After crossing the Big Thompson River the trailhead, the hike follows the western edge of Moraine Park, making it an excellent place for viewing wildlife. Cub Lake is also a great destination for winter hikers, snowshoers, and cross-country skiers. Considered a moderately challenging route the trail can be rocky, so be careful.

Hidden Valley Sledding and Tubing Hill. The only place in Rocky Mountain National Park where sledding is allowed is on the hill at Hidden Valley. Located on the east side of the park about 7 miles from the Beaver Meadows and Fall River Entrance Stations. To go sledding you are on your own and at your own risk.

The Lake Irene Picnic Area is a perfect spot to enjoy Rocky Mountain National Park's alpine area. There are several picnic tables available. After your picnic, walk the 0.5-mile loop around Lake Irene and look at the wildflowers, alpine fir, and Engelmann spruce trees. Directly across Trail Ridge Road from the picnic area is Sheep Rock. Look closely at the top of Sheep Rock and you may find Bighorn Sheep.

Upper Beaver Meadows Trailhead. Birds and other animals are plentiful on this trail and easy to spot. You will hike through an open meadow and Longs Peak looms overhead. After a short walk through the meadow, you will enter the woods. Where you can get views of Longs Peak and Deer Mountain. The trail has some washout ruts, but elevation changes are minimal. Enjoy this 1.1-mile loop trail, considered to be an easy route.

The Loch is one of three spectacular lakes in the scenic Loch Vale area. The 3.1 miles one-way hike to the Loch Lake is a moderate hike. Hikers will walk through aspen groves and cross two bridges that lead to Alberta Falls. Switchbacks are common on this trail and lead hikers through an impressively scenic gorge. Upon reaching the Loch Lake, you will be surrounded by awesome peaks and glaciers.

Twin Sisters Peaks are roughly 11,428 feet high. The hike to Twin Sisters Peak is challenging but rewarding. This hike features a mostly forested trail, with landslide areas, and steep switchbacks. The final trail requires some rock climbing to reach the top of Twin Sisters Peak. From the peak, you can enjoy wonderful views of Longs Peak, Mount Meeker, and Estes Cone. Hiking Distance is 7.4 miles round trip and considered a challenging and strenuous trail.

The Glacier Gorge trail is one of the most popular in Rocky Mountains. This area has multiple trails ranging in difficulty. The trails are great for viewing cascading waterfalls, alpine lakes, and stunning granite cliffs. Glacier Gorge Trailhead has numerous out and back hikes. Hikers will find connecting trails to Bear Lake, as well Glacier Gorge. The length of these trails varies. Glacier Gorge along with other areas were shaped and dredged from glaciers during the last ice age.

Farview Curve Overlook. Enjoy views of the Kawnueeche Valley and the Never Summer Range from this awesome overlook. Along the far side of the valley. You can view the Never Summer Range mountains. This row of mountains is the only volcanic mountain range in Rocky Mountain National Park. This overlook is located along Trail Ridge Road. This road may be closed in the winter months, due to heavy snows. Best time to visit and drive the road is June to September.

Mount Ida Trail is a stunning hike that offers expansive views of Rocky Mountain National Park. This hike is deceiving because it starts out around Poudre Lake with awesome views. Then the uphill climb begins with a 3-thousand-foot elevation gain. Where you will experience all different types of terrain and hiking challenges, including rocks, ice and snow. Hiking Distance is 9.8 miles out-and-back. It is a challenging and strenuous hike. Mount Ida is 12,874 feet tall.

Forest Canyon Overlook. Get a panoramic view of the mountains at 11,716 feet. Or you can take a five-minute walk down the paved asphalt trail to see Forest Canyon, Hayden Gorge, and Gorge Lakes. Here a glacier with grinding force, dredged the valley into the distinctive U-shaped valley. The raw power of a glacier is amazing.

Chapel on the Rock is a stoic chapel perched atop a sacred rock. For 85 years the Chapel on the Rock has survived weather hardships, fires, and floods. Chapel on the Rock is set in a beautiful landscape with majestic mountain peaks and dense forest landscape. It is also a miraculous representation of expertise stonework and craftsmanship. Once you visit it is easy to see why it is one of the most visited chapels.

Facts About Rocky Mountain National Park

1. Rocky Mountain National Park has over 60 mountain peaks that are over 12 thousand feet high. That's 2.7 miles high.

2. The 30-mile-long Continental Divide Trail runs right through the middle of the park, splitting it into its Eastern and Western sections of the park.

3. The park has the country's highest paved road, the Trail Ridge Road. Its highest point is 12,183 ft.

4. The tallest mountain peak in the park is Longs Peak. Sitting at 14,259 ft. It is one of the more difficult ones to summit.

5. Bighorn sheep are the Rockies mascot. The Rockies is home to about 400 bighorn sheep. Due to their presence, they've become known as the National Park's symbol.

6. Altitude Sickness. One in five people visiting elevations above 6,000 feet or higher for the first time develop at least some symptoms of Altitude Sickness.

Things to do in Rocky Mountain National Park

1. **Visitor Centers.** Beaver Meadows, Fall Rivers, Moraine Park, Alpine, Kawuneeche. Moraine Park museum. Holzwarth Historic Site.

2. **Scenic Drives.** Trail Ridge Road. Old Fall River Road.

3. **Hiking.** There are 355 miles of hiking trails.

4. **Camping.** They have 5 campgrounds, or you can do a wilderness overnight camping trip.

5. **Picnicking.** There are many picnic areas throughout the park.

6. **Ranger-led Programs.** You can learn about the park.

7. **Fishing.** There are 50 lakes and streams to fish.

8. **Horseback Riding**. Take a horseback ride to see the park.

9. **Touring in the Park.** Both guided driving and hiking tours are available. Or you can drive vehicles, bicycles, and motorcycles. Permits are required.

Always Plan in Advance Before Going.

Author Page

Billy Grinslott & Kinsey Marie Books

National Parks Books.com

ISBN – 9781965098127

Thanks

www.ingramcontent.com/pod-product-compliance
Lightning Source LLC
LaVergne TN
LVHW070156110826
845147LV00002B/423

* 9 7 8 1 9 6 0 6 1 2 9 6 0 *